First Facts®

ANCIENT EGYPT

HIEROGLYPHS

BY KREMENA SPENGLER

Consultant:
Leo Depuydt
Professor, Department of Egyptology
and Ancient Western Asian Studies
Brown University,
Providence, Rhode Island

Capstone
press

Mankato, Minnesota

First Facts are published by Capstone Press,
151 Good Counsel Drive, P.O. Box 669, Mankato, Minnesota 56002.
www.capstonepress.com

Library of Congress Cataloging-in-Publication Data
Spengler, Kremena.
Hieroglyphs / by Kremena Spengler.
    p. cm. — (First facts. Ancient Egypt)
    Summary: "Describes the ancient Egyptians' hieroglyphic writing system, including types of glyphs, numbers,
and Champollion's discovery of how to read hieroglyphs" — Provided by publisher.
    Includes bibliographical references and index.
    ISBN-13: 978-1-4296-1917-2 (hardcover)
    ISBN-10: 1-4296-1917-1 (hardcover)
    1. Egyptian language — Writing, Hieroglyphic — Juvenile literature. I. Title.
PJ1097.S65 2009
493'.111 — dc22   j493 SPE   OCLC 9/25/09 Gift   2007050992

Editorial Credits

Jennifer Besel, editor; Alison Thiele, designer; Wanda Winch, photo researcher;
    Marcy Morin, page 21 project production

Photo Credits

AP Images/Ben Margot, 4–5; Art Life Images/J.D. Dallet, 14–15; Capstone Press/Karon Dubke, 21; Getty
Images Inc./The Bridgeman Art Library/Egyptian, 11; Getty Images Inc./Photographer's Choice/Ian Mckinnell,
16; Getty Images Inc./Robert Harding World Imagery, 20; Getty Images Inc./Time & Life Pictures/Mansell, 19;
The Image Works/Topham/Werner Forman Archive/Egyptian Museum, Cairo. Location: 47, 13 (left);
iStockphoto/Styve Reineck, 1; New York Public Library/ Astor, Lenox and Tilden Foundations, Asian and Middle
Eastern Division, 17; Photos.com, 18–19; Shutterstock/Alex Brosa, 10; Shutterstock/Asadur Elmokyan, 6
(scroll background), 9; Shutterstock/Baloncici, cover; Shutterstock/Timur Kulgarin, 13 (right); Shutterstock/
YKh, background throughout

Essential content terms are bold and are defined at the bottom of the page where they first appear.

1 2 3 4 5 6 13 12 11 10 09 08

TABLE OF CONTENTS

Egyptian hieroglyphs
made around 2500 BC

4

PICTURES THAT TALK

Imagine a world without letters. Could you write your thoughts down? The ancient Egyptians could. They used pictures instead of letters. These writings are called **hieroglyphs**. Scientists study hieroglyphs to learn about life long ago.

hieroglyph: a picture or sign used in ancient Egyptian writing

ANCIENT EGYPT

The time in history called ancient Egypt began around 3000 BC, about 5,000 years ago. It ended in 30 BC, when Rome took over Egypt.

THE HIEROGLYPHIC ALPHABET
PICTURES THAT STAND FOR SOUNDS

ah father	**p** pop	**h** ha!	**k** kettle
i bill	**f** feet	**kh** lock	**g** good
ee easy	**m** mom	**k** lick	**t** toe
a car	**n** no	**s** see	**ch** church
oo too *or* **w** well	**r** roll	**sh** ship	**d** day
b boy	**h** hand	**q** Iraq	**j** jazz

PICTURE WRITING

Egyptians used different types of hieroglyphs in their writing. Some symbols stand for the objects they look like. A picture of an eye means "eye." Other symbols stand for sounds from the spoken language. The Egyptian word for mouth was said with an "r" sound. In writing, a picture of a mouth stands for that same sound.

NUMBERS

Some hieroglyphs are numbers. Ancient Egyptians didn't have a sign for every number. They combined signs to add up to the correct amount. A vertical line stands for the number one. A rainbow shape represents the number 10. To write the number 32, **scribes** drew three rainbows and two lines.

scribe: a person in ancient Egypt who wrote for other people

HIEROGLYPHIC NUMBERS

	1			2				3			4				5
			6					7					8				9	∩ 10
100	1,000	10,000	100,000	1,000,000

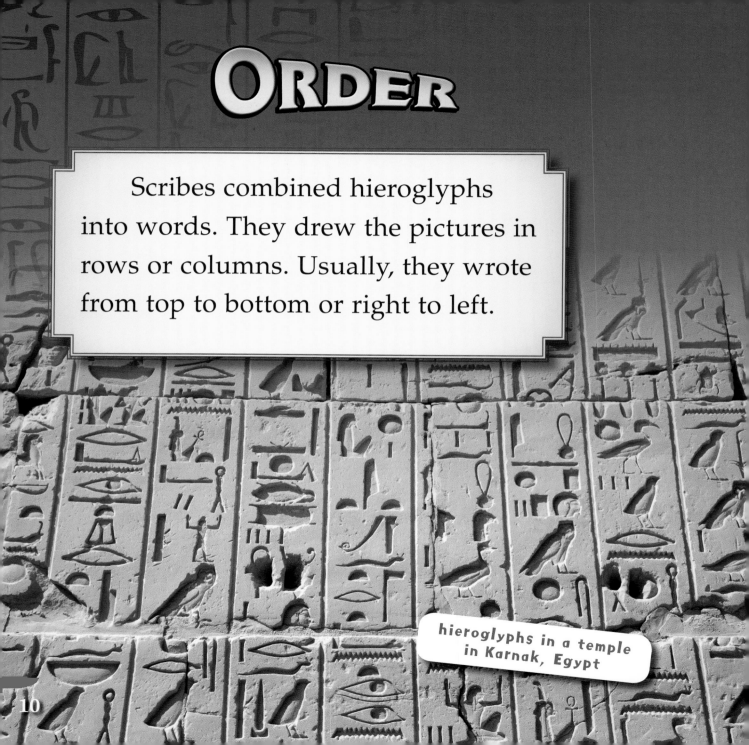

ORDER

Scribes combined hieroglyphs into words. They drew the pictures in rows or columns. Usually, they wrote from top to bottom or right to left.

hieroglyphs in a temple in Karnak, Egypt

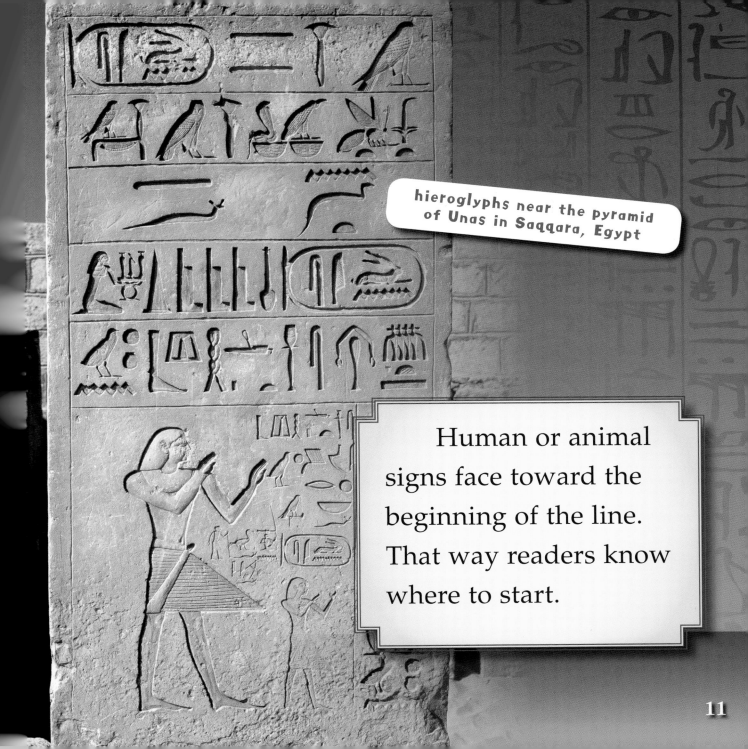

Human or animal signs face toward the beginning of the line. That way readers know where to start.

WRITING MATERIALS

Scribes used reed brushes to write. They cut reeds from the banks of the Nile River. Then they chewed the ends to make brushes. Scribes used black and red ink. Ink was made from plants or ashes. Records were written on **papyrus**. Ink wouldn't fade quickly on papyrus. Scribes also wrote on stone.

papyrus: a material made from reeds that can be written on

DISCOVER!

Students learning to be scribes practiced on broken pieces of pottery.

hieroglyphs on
papyrus

MAKING PAPYRUS

The Egyptians left no record of how they made papyrus. In 1965, Hassan Ragab discovered how to make it the way the Egyptians did. He found that they pressed layers of papyrus fibers together. The pressing squeezed out water and made the fibers flat. Once the fibers were dry, they could be written on. Today, people make papyrus in a factory near the Nile River.

13

DISCOVER!

The ancient Egyptian word for hieroglyphic writing meant "language of the gods."

POWERFUL WRITING

Egyptians believed that writing had magical powers. Scribes painted hieroglyphs on coffins and tomb walls. Ancient Egyptians believed these spells would give the dead everything they needed in the **afterlife**.

afterlife: the place where Egyptians believed a person went after death

FAMOUS HIEROGLYPHS

Much of the ancient Egyptians' writings are spells for those who died. The Pyramid Texts were carved inside pyramids where kings were laid to rest.

text from the pyramid of Teti

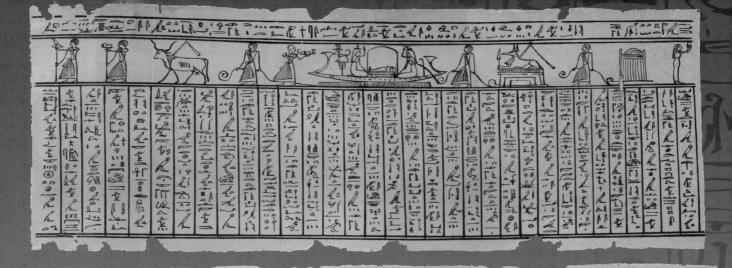

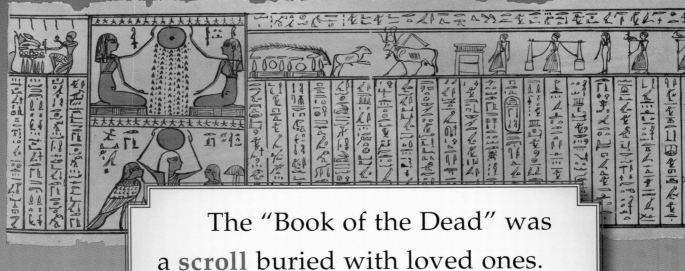

The "Book of the Dead" was a **scroll** buried with loved ones. It included spells a dead person needed to be with the gods.

scroll: a roll of papyrus with writing on it

17

BREAKING THE CODE

Over time, the Egyptians developed a new writing system. Eventually, no one knew how to read hieroglyphs anymore. In 1822, Jean-Francois Champollion broke the code. He used the Rosetta Stone to help figure out the symbols. Today, scientists can read the symbols to learn about the past.

ROSETTA STONE

In 1799, French soldiers found an important stone in Egypt. The stone had the same words written in three writing systems. One was in hieroglyphs. Another one was a newer form of Egyptian. The third one was Greek. Champollion used the stone and his knowledge of language to figure out the hieroglyphs.

Jean-Francois Champollion

19

Scribes in ancient Egypt were highly respected. They had good jobs. Scribes kept records for tax collectors or the king. But learning the job was not easy. Scribes had to know more than 700 hieroglyphs. Only one person out of a hundred Egyptians knew how to write hieroglyphs.

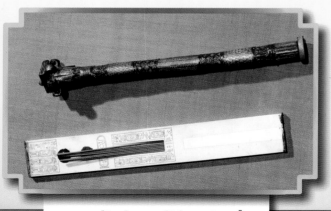

a scribe's writing tools

Hands On: A Cartouche

Scribes made an oval shape around hieroglyphs that spelled out an important person's name. This oval is called a cartouche (kar-TOOSH). You're an important person! You can make a cartouche for yourself.

What You Need

+ red or black marker
+ poster board

What You Do

1. Go to page 6 and look at the hieroglyphs that stand for sounds.

2. Draw the signs that spell your name on the poster board. Remember to draw them from right to left. You might have to skip vowels or sounds that the ancient Egyptians didn't use in their writing.

3. Draw an oval around the symbols you drew.

GLOSSARY

afterlife (AF-tur-life) — the place where Egyptians believed a person's soul went after death

hieroglyph (HYE-ruh-glif) — a symbol used in ancient Egyptian writing

papyrus (puh-PYE-ruhss) — a tall water plant that grows in northern Africa and southern Europe; a material that is written on can be made from the stems of this plant.

scribe (SKRIBE) — a writer in ancient Egypt trained to read and write hieroglyphs

scroll (SKROHL) — a roll of papyrus with writing on it

READ MORE

Parkinson, Richard. *The Pocket Guide to Ancient Egyptian Hieroglyphs*. Pocket Guides. London: British Museum Press, 2004.

Roehrig, Catharine. *Fun with Hieroglyphs*. New York: Metropolitan Museum of Art: Simon and Schuster, 2008.

Strachan, Bruce. *Ancient Egypt: A First Look at People of the Nile*. New York: Henry Holt, 2006.

INTERNET SITES

FactHound offers a safe, fun way to find Internet sites related to this book. All of the sites on FactHound have been researched by our staff.

Here's how:
1. Visit *www.facthound.com*
2. Choose your grade level.
3. Type in this book ID **1429619171** for age-appropriate sites. You may also browse subjects by clicking on letters, or by clicking on pictures and words.
4. Click on the **Fetch It** button.

FactHound will fetch the best sites for you!

INDEX